DIABETIC
DESSERT
COOKBOOK

LIAM LUXE

Copyright © 2024 Liam Luxe

All rights reserved.

CONTENTS

FRUIT-BASED DESSERTS

- Sugar-Free Berry Parfait
- Grilled Pineapple with Cinnamon
- Apple Cinnamon Crisp with Oat Topping
- Poached Pears with Greek Yogurt
- Mixed Fruit Salad with Mint Syrup
- Baked Apples Stuffed with Walnuts and Raisins
- Mango Coconut Chia Pudding
- Peach and Almond Crumble
- Citrus Fruit Sorbet
- Strawberry Banana "Nice" Cream

CHOCOLATE DELIGHTS

- Dark Chocolate Avocado Mousse
- Sugar-Free Chocolate Chip Cookies
- Chocolate Covered Strawberries
- Cocoa Almond Energy Bites
- Chocolate Raspberry Chia Pudding
- Black Bean Brownies
- Chocolate-Dipped Coconut Macaroons
- Chocolate Zucchini Bread
- Chocolate Peanut Butter Cups
- Chocolate Almond Bark with Sea Salt

NUTTY TREATS

Almond Flour Lemon Bars

  Walnut and Date Energy Balls

  Peanut Butter Banana Bites

  Pistachio Apricot Biscotti

  Almond Joy Bites

  Cashew Coconut Bliss Balls

  Homemade Hazelnut Chocolate Spread

  Pecan Pie Bars

  Macadamia Nut Cookies

  Cashew Vanilla Ice Cream

DAIRY-FREE DELIGHTS

  Coconut Flour Pancakes with Berries

  Dairy-Free Vanilla Pudding

  Vegan Carrot Cake Cupcakes

  Coconut Milk Rice Pudding

  Dairy-Free Chocolate Ice Cream

  Vegan Pumpkin Pie

  Tofu Cheesecake with Berry Compote

  Avocado Lime Tart

  Dairy-Free Banana Bread

  Vegan Chocolate Mousse Pie

LOW-CARB CREATIONS

  Keto Lemon Cheesecake Bites

  Low-Carb Blueberry Muffins

  Sugar-Free Coconut Cream Pie

  Avocado Chocolate Pudding

Low-Carb Cheesecake Brownies

Keto-Friendly Chocolate Chip Cookies

Almond Flour Zucchini Bread

Pumpkin Spice Chia Pudding

Low-Carb Strawberry Shortcake

Sugar-Free Cheesecake with Raspberry Sauce

INTERNATIONAL FLAVORS

Greek Yogurt Honey Baklava Bites

Japanese Matcha Green Tea Popsicles

Indian Mango Lassi Smoothie

Italian Affogato with Sugar-Free Espresso

Mexican Spiced Chocolate Avocado Mousse

French Raspberry Clafoutis

Thai Coconut Mango Sticky Rice

Brazilian Açaí Bowl

Middle Eastern Orange Blossom Rice Pudding

Chinese Five-Spice Poached Pears

MEASUREMENT CONVERSION

FRUIT-BASED DESSERTS

SUGAR-FREE BERRY PARFAIT

- **Servings:** 2
- **Time:** 10 minutes

Ingredients:

- 1 cup mixed berries (such as strawberries, blueberries, and raspberries)
- 1 cup Greek yogurt (unsweetened)
- 1 tablespoon chia seeds
- 1 teaspoon vanilla extract
- Stevia or monk fruit sweetener, to taste (optional)
- Fresh mint leaves for garnish (optional)

Instructions:

1. Wash and dry the mixed berries. Slice the strawberries if desired.
2. In a small bowl, mix the Greek yogurt, chia seeds, and vanilla extract. Sweeten with stevia or monk fruit sweetener if desired.
3. Take two serving glasses or bowls. Begin layering the parfait by spooning a dollop of the yogurt mixture into the bottom of each glass.
4. Add a layer of mixed berries on top of the yogurt.
5. Repeat the layers until the glasses are filled, ending with a layer of berries on top.
6. Garnish with fresh mint leaves if desired.
7. Serve immediately or refrigerate until ready to enjoy.

GRILLED PINEAPPLE WITH CINNAMON

- **Servings:** 4
- **Time:** 15 minutes

Ingredients:

- 1 pineapple, peeled and cored
- 1 tablespoon coconut oil, melted
- 1 teaspoon ground cinnamon
- Stevia or monk fruit sweetener, to taste (optional)
- Fresh mint leaves for garnish (optional)

Instructions:

1. Preheat your grill to medium-high heat.
2. Cut the pineapple into slices or wedges, about 1/2 inch thick.

3. In a small bowl, mix together the melted coconut oil and ground cinnamon.
4. Brush both sides of each pineapple slice with the cinnamon-coconut oil mixture.
5. Place the pineapple slices on the preheated grill and cook for 2-3 minutes on each side, or until grill marks appear and the pineapple caramelizes slightly.
6. Remove the grilled pineapple from the grill and transfer to a serving platter.
7. Sweeten with stevia or monk fruit sweetener if desired.
8. Garnish with fresh mint leaves if desired.

APPLE CINNAMON CRISP WITH OAT TOPPING

- **Servings:** 6
- **Time:** 45 minutes

Ingredients:

- 4 medium apples, peeled, cored, and sliced
- 1 tablespoon lemon juice
- 1 teaspoon ground cinnamon
- 2 tablespoons stevia or monk fruit sweetener
- 1/2 cup old-fashioned oats
- 1/4 cup almond flour
- 2 tablespoons coconut oil, melted
- 1/4 cup chopped nuts (such as walnuts or pecans), optional
- Pinch of salt

Instructions:

1. Preheat your oven to 350°F (175°C). Grease a baking dish with coconut oil or non-stick cooking spray.
2. In a large bowl, toss the sliced apples with lemon juice, ground cinnamon, and stevia or monk fruit sweetener until well coated. Transfer the apple mixture to the prepared baking dish and spread it out evenly.
3. In the same bowl (no need to wash), combine the old-fashioned oats, almond flour, melted coconut oil, chopped nuts (if using), and a pinch of salt. Mix until the mixture resembles coarse crumbs.
4. Spread the oat topping evenly over the apple mixture in the baking dish.
5. Bake in the preheated oven for 30-35 minutes, or until the topping is golden brown and the apples are tender.
6. Remove from the oven and let cool for a few minutes before serving.
7. Serve warm as is or with a dollop of Greek yogurt or a scoop of sugar-free vanilla ice cream for an extra treat.

POACHED PEARS WITH GREEK YOGURT

- **Servings:** 4
- **Time:** 30 minutes

Ingredients:

- 4 ripe pears, peeled and cored
- 2 cups water
- 1/2 cup unsweetened apple juice
- 1 cinnamon stick
- 1 teaspoon vanilla extract
- 2 tablespoons stevia or monk fruit sweetener
- 1 cup Greek yogurt (unsweetened)

- Ground cinnamon, for garnish (optional)
- Chopped nuts or granola, for garnish (optional)

Instructions:

1. In a large saucepan, combine the water, unsweetened apple juice, cinnamon stick, vanilla extract, and stevia or monk fruit sweetener. Bring the mixture to a simmer over medium heat.
2. Add the peeled and cored pears to the simmering liquid. Cover and let them simmer gently for about 20-25 minutes, or until the pears are tender when pierced with a fork.
3. Once the pears are tender, remove them from the poaching liquid using a slotted spoon and transfer them to a serving dish. Discard the cinnamon stick.
4. Allow the poaching liquid to continue simmering until it reduces and thickens slightly, about 5-10 minutes more. This will create a syrupy sauce.
5. To serve, place a poached pear on each plate and drizzle with some of the poaching syrup.
6. Add a dollop of Greek yogurt on the side of each pear.
7. Sprinkle ground cinnamon over the pears and yogurt for extra flavor if desired.
8. Garnish with chopped nuts or granola if desired.

MIXED FRUIT SALAD WITH MINT SYRUP

- **Servings:** 4
- **Time:** 15 minutes

Ingredients:

- 2 cups mixed fresh fruits (such as strawberries, blueberries, grapes, kiwi, and oranges), washed and chopped
- 2 tablespoons fresh mint leaves, chopped
- 1 tablespoon lemon juice
- 2 tablespoons honey or maple syrup
- 1/4 teaspoon vanilla extract

Instructions:

1. In a large mixing bowl, combine the chopped mixed fruits and fresh mint leaves.
2. In a small bowl, whisk together the lemon juice, honey or maple syrup, and vanilla extract to make the mint syrup.
3. Pour the mint syrup over the mixed fruits and gently toss until well combined.
4. Allow the fruit salad to marinate in the refrigerator for about 10 minutes to let the flavors meld together.
5. Once ready to serve, divide the fruit salad into serving bowls or plates.
6. Garnish with additional fresh mint leaves if desired.

BAKED APPLES STUFFED WITH WALNUTS AND RAISINS

- **Servings:** 4
- **Time:** 45 minutes

Ingredients:

- 4 large apples (such as Granny Smith or Honeycrisp), washed and cored
- 1/4 cup walnuts, chopped

- 1/4 cup raisins
- 2 tablespoons honey or maple syrup
- 1 teaspoon ground cinnamon
- 1/4 teaspoon ground nutmeg
- 1 tablespoon lemon juice
- 1 tablespoon water

Instructions:

1. Preheat your oven to 375°F (190°C). Grease a baking dish with coconut oil or non-stick cooking spray.
2. In a small bowl, mix together the chopped walnuts, raisins, honey or maple syrup, ground cinnamon, and ground nutmeg until well combined.
3. Place the cored apples in the prepared baking dish.
4. Stuff each apple with the walnut and raisin mixture, pressing gently to fill the cavity.
5. Drizzle the lemon juice over the stuffed apples.
6. Pour the water into the bottom of the baking dish to prevent the apples from sticking.
7. Cover the baking dish with foil and bake in the preheated oven for 25-30 minutes, or until the apples are tender when pierced with a fork.
8. Remove the foil during the last 5 minutes of baking to allow the tops of the apples to brown slightly.
9. Once baked, remove the apples from the oven and let them cool for a few minutes before serving.
10. Serve the baked apples warm, either as is or with a dollop of Greek yogurt or a sprinkle of additional cinnamon on top.

MANGO COCONUT CHIA PUDDING

- **Servings:** 2
- **Time:** 4 hours (includes chilling time)

Ingredients:

- 1 ripe mango, peeled and diced
- 1/2 cup coconut milk
- 2 tablespoons chia seeds
- 1 tablespoon honey or maple syrup (optional, depending on sweetness of mango)
- 1/2 teaspoon vanilla extract

Instructions:

1. In a blender or food processor, puree the diced mango until smooth.
2. In a mixing bowl, combine the mango puree, coconut milk, chia seeds, honey or maple syrup (if using), and vanilla extract. Stir well to combine.
3. Cover the bowl and refrigerate for at least 4 hours or overnight, allowing the chia seeds to absorb the liquid and thicken the pudding.
4. After chilling, give the pudding a good stir to redistribute the chia seeds evenly.
5. Divide the mango coconut chia pudding into serving glasses or bowls.
6. Optional: Garnish with additional diced mango or shredded coconut on top.

PEACH AND ALMOND CRUMBLE

- **Servings:** 6
- **Time:** 45 minutes

Ingredients:

- 6 ripe peaches, peeled, pitted, and sliced
- 1 tablespoon lemon juice
- 1/4 cup granulated stevia or monk fruit sweetener
- 1/2 teaspoon ground cinnamon
- 1/4 teaspoon ground nutmeg
- 1/2 cup almond flour
- 1/4 cup old-fashioned oats
- 1/4 cup chopped almonds
- 2 tablespoons coconut oil, melted
- 2 tablespoons honey or maple syrup
- Pinch of salt

Instructions:

1. Preheat your oven to 350°F (175°C). Grease a baking dish with coconut oil or non-stick cooking spray.
2. In a large bowl, combine the sliced peaches with lemon juice, granulated stevia or monk fruit sweetener, ground cinnamon, and ground nutmeg. Toss until the peaches are evenly coated.
3. Transfer the peach mixture to the prepared baking dish, spreading it out evenly.
4. In the same bowl, mix together the almond flour, old-fashioned oats, chopped almonds, melted coconut oil, honey or maple syrup, and a pinch of salt until well combined.
5. Sprinkle the almond-oat mixture evenly over the top of the peaches in the baking dish.
6. Bake in the preheated oven for 30-35 minutes, or until the peach filling is bubbling and the crumble topping is golden brown and crisp.

7. Remove from the oven and let cool for a few minutes before serving.
8. Serve warm as is or with a scoop of sugar-free vanilla ice cream or a dollop of Greek yogurt for an extra treat.

CITRUS FRUIT SORBET

- **Servings:** 4
- **Time:** 4 hours (includes freezing time)

Ingredients:

- 2 cups mixed citrus juice (such as orange, lemon, and lime)
- 1/2 cup water
- 1/2 cup granulated stevia or monk fruit sweetener
- Zest of one citrus fruit (optional, for extra flavor)

Instructions:

1. In a small saucepan, combine the water and granulated stevia or monk fruit sweetener. Heat over medium heat, stirring occasionally, until the sweetener is completely dissolved. Remove from heat and let it cool.
2. In a large mixing bowl, combine the mixed citrus juice with the cooled sweetened water. If using citrus zest, add it to the bowl and mix well.
3. Pour the citrus mixture into a shallow baking dish or a freezer-safe container.
4. Place the dish or container in the freezer and let it freeze for about 2-3 hours, or until the mixture begins to solidify around the edges.

5. Remove the partially frozen mixture from the freezer and use a fork to break up any ice crystals that have formed.
6. Return the mixture to the freezer and continue to freeze for another 2-3 hours, or until it is completely frozen.
7. Once fully frozen, remove the sorbet from the freezer and let it sit at room temperature for a few minutes to soften slightly.
8. Use a fork to scrape the surface of the sorbet to create a fluffy texture.
9. Serve the citrus fruit sorbet in chilled bowls or glasses.
10. Garnish with additional citrus zest or fresh mint leaves if desired.

STRAWBERRY BANANA "NICE" CREAM

- **Servings:** 2
- **Time:** 10 minutes

Ingredients:

- 2 ripe bananas, peeled, sliced, and frozen
- 1 cup frozen strawberries
- 1/4 cup unsweetened almond milk or coconut milk
- 1 teaspoon vanilla extract
- Stevia or monk fruit sweetener, to taste (optional)

Instructions:

1. Place the frozen banana slices, frozen strawberries, almond milk or coconut milk, and vanilla extract in a blender or food processor.
2. If desired, add stevia or monk fruit sweetener to sweeten the "nice" cream.

3. Blend the ingredients on high speed until smooth and creamy, scraping down the sides of the blender or food processor as needed.
4. If the mixture is too thick, add more almond milk or coconut milk, a tablespoon at a time, until the desired consistency is reached.
5. Once smooth, transfer the strawberry banana "nice" cream to serving bowls.
6. Optional: Garnish with additional sliced strawberries or banana slices on top.

CHOCOLATE DELIGHTS

DARK CHOCOLATE AVOCADO MOUSSE

- **Servings:** 4
- **Time:** 15 minutes

Ingredients:

- 2 ripe avocados, peeled and pitted
- 1/4 cup unsweetened cocoa powder
- 1/4 cup maple syrup or honey
- 1 teaspoon vanilla extract
- Pinch of salt
- 1/4 cup almond milk or coconut milk, as needed for consistency
- Dark chocolate shavings or cocoa powder, for garnish (optional)

Instructions:

1. In a blender or food processor, combine the ripe avocados, unsweetened cocoa powder, maple syrup or honey, vanilla extract, and a pinch of salt.
2. Blend the ingredients until smooth and creamy, scraping down the sides of the blender or food processor as needed.
3. If the mixture is too thick, add almond milk or coconut milk, a tablespoon at a time, until the desired consistency is reached.
4. Taste the mousse and adjust the sweetness if necessary by adding more maple syrup or honey.
5. Once smooth and creamy, transfer the dark chocolate avocado mousse to serving bowls or glasses.
6. Optional: Garnish with dark chocolate shavings or a sprinkle of cocoa powder on top.

SUGAR-FREE CHOCOLATE CHIP COOKIES

- **Servings:** 12 cookies
- **Time:** 20 minutes

Ingredients:

- 1 cup almond flour
- 1/4 cup coconut flour
- 1/4 teaspoon baking soda
- 1/4 teaspoon salt
- 1/4 cup coconut oil, melted
- 1/4 cup sugar-free maple syrup or erythritol-based sweetener
- 1 teaspoon vanilla extract

- 1/4 cup sugar-free dark chocolate chips

Instructions:

1. Preheat your oven to 350°F (175°C). Line a baking sheet with parchment paper or silicone baking mat.
2. In a large mixing bowl, whisk together the almond flour, coconut flour, baking soda, and salt until well combined.
3. In a separate bowl, mix together the melted coconut oil, sugar-free maple syrup or sweetener, and vanilla extract until smooth.
4. Pour the wet ingredients into the dry ingredients and stir until a dough forms.
5. Fold in the sugar-free dark chocolate chips until evenly distributed throughout the dough.
6. Use a cookie scoop or spoon to portion out the dough and place them onto the prepared baking sheet, spacing them apart.
7. Flatten each cookie slightly with the back of a spoon or your fingertips.
8. Bake in the preheated oven for 10-12 minutes, or until the edges are golden brown.
9. Remove from the oven and let the cookies cool on the baking sheet for a few minutes before transferring them to a wire rack to cool completely.

CHOCOLATE COVERED STRAWBERRIES

- **Servings:** 12 strawberries
- **Time:** 30 minutes

Ingredients:

- 12 large strawberries, washed and dried
- 4 ounces sugar-free dark chocolate, chopped
- 1 teaspoon coconut oil
- Optional toppings: chopped nuts, shredded coconut, sprinkles

Instructions:

1. Line a baking sheet with parchment paper or wax paper.
2. In a heatproof bowl, combine the chopped sugar-free dark chocolate and coconut oil.
3. Microwave the chocolate in 30-second intervals, stirring in between, until completely melted and smooth. Alternatively, you can melt the chocolate using a double boiler on the stove.
4. Hold each strawberry by the stem and dip it into the melted chocolate, swirling to coat evenly.
5. Allow any excess chocolate to drip off, then place the chocolate-covered strawberry onto the prepared baking sheet.
6. Repeat the dipping process with the remaining strawberries.
7. Optional: While the chocolate is still wet, sprinkle the chocolate-covered strawberries with chopped nuts, shredded coconut, or sprinkles for added flavor and decoration.
8. Once all the strawberries are coated, place the baking sheet in the refrigerator for about 15-20 minutes, or until the chocolate sets.
9. Once set, remove the chocolate-covered strawberries from the refrigerator and serve immediately, or store them in an airtight container in the refrigerator for up to 2 days.

COCOA ALMOND ENERGY BITES

- **Servings:** 12 energy bites
- **Time:** 15 minutes

Ingredients:

- 1 cup rolled oats
- 1/2 cup almond butter
- 1/4 cup cocoa powder
- 1/4 cup honey or maple syrup
- 1/4 cup chopped almonds
- 1 teaspoon vanilla extract
- Pinch of salt
- Optional: shredded coconut, chia seeds, or mini chocolate chips for coating

Instructions:

1. In a large mixing bowl, combine the rolled oats, almond butter, cocoa powder, honey or maple syrup, chopped almonds, vanilla extract, and a pinch of salt.
2. Stir the ingredients together until well combined. If the mixture is too dry, you can add a little more almond butter or honey/maple syrup to help bind it together.
3. Once the mixture is well combined and holds together easily, use your hands to roll it into small balls, about 1 inch in diameter.
4. Optional: Roll the energy bites in shredded coconut, chia seeds, or mini chocolate chips for additional flavor and texture.
5. Place the rolled energy bites on a baking sheet lined with parchment paper.

6. Refrigerate the energy bites for at least 30 minutes to firm up.
7. Once firm, transfer the cocoa almond energy bites to an airtight container and store them in the refrigerator for up to 1 week.

CHOCOLATE RASPBERRY CHIA PUDDING

- **Servings:** 2
- **Time:** 4 hours (includes chilling time)

Ingredients:

- 1 cup unsweetened almond milk or coconut milk
- 1/4 cup chia seeds
- 2 tablespoons cocoa powder
- 2 tablespoons honey or maple syrup
- 1/2 teaspoon vanilla extract
- 1/2 cup fresh raspberries, plus extra for garnish
- Optional: shredded coconut or chopped nuts for garnish

Instructions:

1. In a mixing bowl, combine the unsweetened almond milk or coconut milk, chia seeds, cocoa powder, honey or maple syrup, and vanilla extract. Whisk until well combined.
2. Allow the mixture to sit for a few minutes, then whisk again to prevent clumps from forming.
3. Gently fold in the fresh raspberries, using a spoon to crush some of the raspberries and release their juices.
4. Divide the chocolate raspberry chia pudding mixture evenly between two serving glasses or jars.

5. Cover the glasses or jars with plastic wrap or lids and refrigerate for at least 4 hours or overnight, allowing the chia seeds to absorb the liquid and thicken the pudding.
6. Once chilled and set, remove the chocolate raspberry chia pudding from the refrigerator.
7. Optional: Garnish with additional fresh raspberries, shredded coconut, or chopped nuts on top.

BLACK BEAN BROWNIES

- **Servings:** 12 brownies
- **Time:** 35 minutes

Ingredients:

- 1 can (15 ounces) black beans, drained and rinsed
- 3 large eggs
- 1/4 cup coconut oil, melted
- 1/2 cup unsweetened cocoa powder
- 1/2 cup honey or maple syrup
- 1 teaspoon vanilla extract
- 1/2 teaspoon baking powder
- Pinch of salt
- 1/4 cup sugar-free dark chocolate chips (optional)

Instructions:

1. Preheat your oven to 350°F (175°C). Grease a 9x9-inch baking pan or line it with parchment paper.
2. In a food processor, combine the black beans, eggs, melted coconut oil, cocoa powder, honey or maple syrup, vanilla extract, baking powder, and a pinch of salt.

3. Blend the ingredients until smooth and well combined, scraping down the sides of the food processor as needed.
4. If using, stir in the sugar-free dark chocolate chips into the batter.
5. Pour the batter into the prepared baking pan and spread it out evenly with a spatula.
6. Bake in the preheated oven for 25-30 minutes, or until the brownies are set and a toothpick inserted into the center comes out clean.
7. Remove from the oven and let the brownies cool in the pan for about 10 minutes before slicing and serving.
8. Once cooled, cut the black bean brownies into squares and enjoy! These brownies are moist, fudgy, and packed with protein and fiber from the black beans, making them a healthier alternative to traditional brownies.

CHOCOLATE-DIPPED COCONUT MACAROONS

- **Servings:** 12 macaroons
- **Time:** 30 minutes

Ingredients:

- 2 cups unsweetened shredded coconut
- 1/2 cup sweetened condensed milk (or coconut condensed milk for dairy-free)
- 1 teaspoon vanilla extract
- 2 large egg whites
- Pinch of salt
- 4 ounces sugar-free dark chocolate, chopped

Instructions:

1. Preheat your oven to 325°F (160°C). Line a baking sheet with parchment paper.
2. In a large mixing bowl, combine the unsweetened shredded coconut, sweetened condensed milk, and vanilla extract. Stir until well combined.
3. In a separate bowl, beat the egg whites and a pinch of salt until stiff peaks form.
4. Gently fold the beaten egg whites into the coconut mixture until fully incorporated.
5. Using a spoon or cookie scoop, portion out the coconut mixture and shape it into small mounds on the prepared baking sheet, leaving space between each macaroon.
6. Bake in the preheated oven for 20-25 minutes, or until the macaroons are golden brown around the edges.
7. Remove the macaroons from the oven and let them cool on the baking sheet for a few minutes before transferring them to a wire rack to cool completely.
8. Once the macaroons are cooled, melt the sugar-free dark chocolate in a heatproof bowl set over a pot of simmering water (double boiler method) or in the microwave in 30-second intervals, stirring in between until smooth.
9. Dip the bottoms of each macaroon into the melted chocolate, then place them back on the parchment paper-lined baking sheet.
10. Optional: Drizzle the remaining melted chocolate over the tops of the macaroons for added decoration.
11. Place the baking sheet in the refrigerator for about 10-15 minutes, or until the chocolate is set.
12. Once set, remove the chocolate-dipped coconut macaroons from the refrigerator and serve.

CHOCOLATE ZUCCHINI BREAD

- **Servings:** 10 slices
- **Time:** 1 hour

Ingredients:

- 1 1/2 cups shredded zucchini (about 1 medium zucchini)
- 1 1/2 cups all-purpose flour
- 1/2 cup unsweetened cocoa powder
- 1 teaspoon baking soda
- 1/2 teaspoon baking powder
- 1/2 teaspoon salt
- 1/2 cup coconut oil, melted
- 3/4 cup honey or maple syrup
- 2 large eggs
- 1 teaspoon vanilla extract
- 1/2 cup sugar-free dark chocolate chips (optional)

Instructions:

1. Preheat your oven to 350°F (175°C). Grease a 9x5-inch loaf pan with coconut oil or line it with parchment paper.
2. Place the shredded zucchini in a clean kitchen towel and squeeze out any excess moisture.
3. In a large mixing bowl, whisk together the all-purpose flour, unsweetened cocoa powder, baking soda, baking powder, and salt.
4. In a separate bowl, whisk together the melted coconut oil, honey or maple syrup, eggs, and vanilla extract until well combined.
5. Pour the wet ingredients into the dry ingredients and stir until just combined. Do not overmix.

6. Fold in the shredded zucchini and sugar-free dark chocolate chips (if using) until evenly distributed throughout the batter.
7. Pour the batter into the prepared loaf pan and spread it out evenly with a spatula.
8. Bake in the preheated oven for 50-60 minutes, or until a toothpick inserted into the center of the bread comes out clean.
9. Remove the chocolate zucchini bread from the oven and let it cool in the pan for about 10 minutes.
10. Once cooled slightly, transfer the bread to a wire rack to cool completely before slicing.

CHOCOLATE PEANUT BUTTER CUPS

- **Servings:** 12 peanut butter cups
- **Time:** 30 minutes

Ingredients:

- 1 cup sugar-free dark chocolate chips
- 1/2 cup natural peanut butter (unsweetened)
- 2 tablespoons coconut oil, divided
- 2 tablespoons powdered erythritol or monk fruit sweetener (optional, for sweetening peanut butter)

Instructions:

1. Line a muffin tin with 12 paper liners or silicone molds.
2. In a microwave-safe bowl, combine the sugar-free dark chocolate chips and 1 tablespoon of coconut oil. Microwave in 30-second intervals, stirring in between, until the chocolate is melted and smooth.

3. Spoon about 1 tablespoon of the melted chocolate mixture into each paper liner, spreading it to cover the bottom and slightly up the sides.
4. Place the muffin tin in the freezer for about 10 minutes to allow the chocolate to firm up.
5. While the chocolate is chilling, in another bowl, mix the natural peanut butter with the remaining 1 tablespoon of coconut oil and powdered erythritol or monk fruit sweetener (if using) until smooth.
6. Remove the muffin tin from the freezer and spoon about 1 teaspoon of the peanut butter mixture into each chocolate-lined cup, spreading it out evenly.
7. Once all cups are filled with peanut butter, spoon the remaining melted chocolate over the top of each cup, covering the peanut butter completely.
8. Return the muffin tin to the freezer for another 10-15 minutes to allow the chocolate to set completely.
9. Once set, remove the chocolate peanut butter cups from the muffin tin and peel off the paper liners or silicone molds.
10. Store the chocolate peanut butter cups in an airtight container in the refrigerator until ready to serve.

CHOCOLATE ALMOND BARK WITH SEA SALT

- **Servings:** 12 servings
- **Time:** 15 minutes (+ setting time)

Ingredients:

- 12 ounces sugar-free dark chocolate, chopped

- 1 cup roasted almonds, roughly chopped
- 1 teaspoon coarse sea salt

Instructions:

1. Line a baking sheet with parchment paper or a silicone baking mat.
2. In a heatproof bowl set over a pot of simmering water (double boiler method) or in the microwave, melt the sugar-free dark chocolate, stirring frequently until smooth.
3. Once melted, remove the chocolate from heat and stir in the chopped roasted almonds until they are evenly coated.
4. Pour the chocolate and almond mixture onto the prepared baking sheet, spreading it out into an even layer with a spatula.
5. Sprinkle the coarse sea salt evenly over the top of the chocolate-almond mixture.
6. Place the baking sheet in the refrigerator for about 30 minutes to 1 hour, or until the chocolate is set and firm.
7. Once set, remove the chocolate almond bark from the refrigerator and break it into smaller pieces.
8. Store the chocolate almond bark in an airtight container in the refrigerator until ready to serve.

NUTTY TREATS

ALMOND FLOUR LEMON BARS

- **Servings:** 12 bars
- **Time:** 45 minutes

Ingredients: *For the Crust:*

- 1 1/2 cups almond flour
- 1/4 cup coconut oil, melted
- 2 tablespoons powdered erythritol or monk fruit sweetener
- Pinch of salt

For the Lemon Filling:

- 3/4 cup fresh lemon juice (about 4-5 lemons)

- Zest of 2 lemons
- 1 cup powdered erythritol or monk fruit sweetener
- 4 large eggs
- 2 tablespoons almond flour
- 1/4 teaspoon baking powder
- Powdered erythritol or monk fruit sweetener, for dusting (optional)

Instructions:

1. Preheat your oven to 350°F (175°C). Grease an 8x8-inch baking dish with coconut oil or line it with parchment paper, leaving some overhang for easy removal.
2. In a mixing bowl, combine the almond flour, melted coconut oil, powdered erythritol or monk fruit sweetener, and a pinch of salt for the crust. Mix until well combined.
3. Press the crust mixture evenly into the bottom of the prepared baking dish.
4. Bake the crust in the preheated oven for 12-15 minutes, or until lightly golden brown around the edges. Remove from the oven and let it cool slightly.
5. In another mixing bowl, whisk together the fresh lemon juice, lemon zest, powdered erythritol or monk fruit sweetener, eggs, almond flour, and baking powder until smooth.
6. Pour the lemon filling over the partially baked crust, spreading it out evenly.
7. Return the baking dish to the oven and bake for an additional 20-25 minutes, or until the filling is set and the edges are golden brown.
8. Remove from the oven and let the lemon bars cool completely in the baking dish.

9. Once cooled, dust the top of the lemon bars with powdered erythritol or monk fruit sweetener, if desired.
10. Using the parchment paper overhang, lift the lemon bars out of the baking dish and transfer them to a cutting board.
11. Slice the lemon bars into squares or rectangles.

WALNUT AND DATE ENERGY BALLS

- **Servings:** 12 energy balls
- **Time:** 15 minutes

Ingredients:

- 1 cup walnuts
- 1 cup pitted dates
- 2 tablespoons unsweetened cocoa powder
- 1 tablespoon coconut oil, melted
- 1 teaspoon vanilla extract
- Pinch of salt
- Optional: shredded coconut or cocoa powder for rolling

Instructions:

1. In a food processor, combine the walnuts, pitted dates, unsweetened cocoa powder, melted coconut oil, vanilla extract, and a pinch of salt.
2. Process the mixture until it forms a sticky dough-like consistency, scraping down the sides of the food processor as needed.
3. Once the mixture is well combined and holds together easily, use your hands to roll it into small balls, about 1 inch in diameter.

4. Optional: Roll the energy balls in shredded coconut or cocoa powder for added flavor and texture.
5. Place the rolled energy balls on a plate or baking sheet lined with parchment paper.
6. Refrigerate the energy balls for at least 30 minutes to firm up.
7. Once firm, transfer the walnut and date energy balls to an airtight container and store them in the refrigerator for up to 1 week.

PEANUT BUTTER BANANA BITES

- **Servings:** 12 bites
- **Time:** 10 minutes

Ingredients:

- 2 ripe bananas
- 1/4 cup peanut butter (or any nut or seed butter of your choice)
- Optional toppings: chopped nuts, shredded coconut, mini chocolate chips, chia seeds

Instructions:

1. Peel the bananas and slice them into rounds, about 1/2 inch thick.
2. Spread a small amount of peanut butter onto one side of each banana slice.
3. Sandwich two banana slices together with the peanut butter side facing inwards, creating banana "sandwiches".

4. Optional: Roll the edges of the banana sandwiches in chopped nuts, shredded coconut, mini chocolate chips, or chia seeds for added flavor and texture.
5. Place the assembled peanut butter banana bites on a plate or baking sheet lined with parchment paper.
6. Repeat the process until all banana slices are used.
7. Serve the peanut butter banana bites immediately, or refrigerate them for about 30 minutes to firm up before serving.

PISTACHIO APRICOT BISCOTTI

- **Servings:** 24 biscotti
- **Time:** 1 hour 30 minutes

Ingredients:

- 2 cups all-purpose flour
- 1 teaspoon baking powder
- 1/4 teaspoon salt
- 1/2 cup unsalted butter, softened
- 3/4 cup granulated sugar
- 2 large eggs
- 1 teaspoon vanilla extract
- 1/2 cup shelled pistachios, roughly chopped
- 1/2 cup dried apricots, chopped

Instructions:

1. Preheat your oven to 350°F (175°C). Line a baking sheet with parchment paper.
2. In a mixing bowl, sift together the all-purpose flour, baking powder, and salt. Set aside.

3. In a separate mixing bowl, cream together the softened unsalted butter and granulated sugar until light and fluffy.
4. Beat in the eggs, one at a time, until well combined. Stir in the vanilla extract.
5. Gradually add the flour mixture to the wet ingredients, mixing until a dough forms.
6. Fold in the chopped pistachios and dried apricots until evenly distributed throughout the dough.
7. Divide the dough in half. Shape each half into a log, about 12 inches long and 2 inches wide, on the prepared baking sheet. Make sure to leave some space between the logs as they will spread during baking.
8. Bake in the preheated oven for 25-30 minutes, or until the logs are firm to the touch and lightly golden brown.
9. Remove the baking sheet from the oven and let the biscotti logs cool for about 10 minutes.
10. Reduce the oven temperature to 325°F (160°C).
11. Carefully transfer the baked logs to a cutting board. Using a sharp knife, slice the logs diagonally into 1/2-inch thick slices.
12. Place the sliced biscotti upright back onto the baking sheet, leaving some space between each slice.
13. Bake the biscotti for an additional 10-15 minutes, or until they are golden and crisp.
14. Remove from the oven and let the biscotti cool completely on the baking sheet.
15. Once cooled, store the pistachio apricot biscotti in an airtight container at room temperature for up to 2 weeks.

ALMOND JOY BITES

- **Servings:** 12 bites
- **Time:** 20 minutes (+ chilling time)

Ingredients:

- 1 cup shredded coconut (unsweetened)
- 1/4 cup almond flour
- 2 tablespoons maple syrup or honey
- 2 tablespoons coconut oil, melted
- 1/2 teaspoon vanilla extract
- 24 whole almonds
- 1/2 cup sugar-free dark chocolate chips

Instructions:

1. In a mixing bowl, combine the shredded coconut, almond flour, maple syrup or honey, melted coconut oil, and vanilla extract. Mix until well combined and the mixture holds together.
2. Using your hands, shape the mixture into small balls, about 1 tablespoon each, and place them on a baking sheet lined with parchment paper.
3. Press one whole almond into the center of each coconut ball, flattening it slightly.
4. Place the baking sheet in the refrigerator for about 30 minutes to allow the coconut balls to firm up.
5. In the meantime, melt the sugar-free dark chocolate chips in a microwave-safe bowl in 30-second intervals, stirring in between, until smooth and melted.
6. Once the coconut balls are firm, remove them from the refrigerator.
7. Using a spoon, drizzle the melted chocolate over the top of each coconut ball, covering the almond partially.

8. Place the baking sheet back in the refrigerator for another 10-15 minutes, or until the chocolate is set.
9. Once set, remove the Almond Joy bites from the refrigerator and serve.

CASHEW COCONUT BLISS BALLS

- **Servings:** 12 bliss balls
- **Time:** 15 minutes (+ chilling time)

Ingredients:

- 1 cup raw cashews
- 1 cup shredded coconut (unsweetened)
- 2 tablespoons coconut oil, melted
- 2 tablespoons maple syrup or honey
- 1 teaspoon vanilla extract
- Pinch of salt
- Additional shredded coconut, for rolling (optional)

Instructions:

1. In a food processor, pulse the raw cashews until they are finely ground into a coarse flour-like consistency.
2. Add the shredded coconut, melted coconut oil, maple syrup or honey, vanilla extract, and a pinch of salt to the food processor.
3. Process the mixture until it comes together into a sticky dough-like consistency.
4. If the mixture is too dry, you can add a little more melted coconut oil or maple syrup to help bind it together.

5. Using your hands, roll the mixture into small balls, about 1 tablespoon each, and place them on a baking sheet lined with parchment paper.
6. Optional: Roll each bliss ball in additional shredded coconut to coat the outside for added texture and flavor.
7. Once all the bliss balls are rolled, place the baking sheet in the refrigerator for about 30 minutes to firm up.
8. Once firm, remove the cashew coconut bliss balls from the refrigerator and serve.

HOMEMADE HAZELNUT CHOCOLATE SPREAD

- **Yield:** About 1 cup
- **Time:** 20 minutes

Ingredients:

- 1 cup raw hazelnuts
- 1/4 cup cocoa powder
- 1/4 cup powdered erythritol or powdered sugar
- 2 tablespoons coconut oil, melted
- 1 teaspoon vanilla extract
- Pinch of salt

Instructions:

1. Preheat your oven to 350°F (175°C). Spread the hazelnuts in a single layer on a baking sheet and roast them for about 10-12 minutes, or until they are fragrant and lightly browned.

2. Remove the hazelnuts from the oven and let them cool slightly. Once cooled, transfer the hazelnuts to a clean kitchen towel and rub them together to remove the skins.
3. Place the peeled hazelnuts in a food processor and process them until they form a smooth and creamy hazelnut butter, scraping down the sides of the processor as needed. This process may take several minutes.
4. Once the hazelnuts have turned into butter, add the cocoa powder, powdered erythritol or powdered sugar, melted coconut oil, vanilla extract, and a pinch of salt to the food processor.
5. Process the mixture until all the ingredients are well combined and the chocolate spread is smooth and creamy.
6. Taste the chocolate spread and adjust the sweetness or cocoa flavor as desired by adding more powdered erythritol or cocoa powder.
7. Once the chocolate spread reaches your desired consistency and flavor, transfer it to a clean jar or airtight container.
8. Store the homemade hazelnut chocolate spread in the refrigerator for up to 2 weeks.
9. Enjoy this delicious spread on toast, pancakes, fruit, or as a dip for pretzels and crackers!

PECAN PIE BARS

- **Servings:** 16 bars
- **Time:** 1 hour 30 minutes (includes cooling time)

Ingredients:

For the Crust:

- 1 1/2 cups all-purpose flour
- 1/2 cup unsalted butter, softened
- 1/4 cup granulated sugar
- Pinch of salt

For the Pecan Filling:

- 3/4 cup packed brown sugar
- 1/2 cup light corn syrup
- 1/4 cup unsalted butter
- 2 large eggs, beaten
- 1 teaspoon vanilla extract
- 1 1/2 cups pecan halves

Instructions:

1. Preheat your oven to 350°F (175°C). Grease or line a 9x9-inch baking pan with parchment paper, leaving some overhang for easy removal.
2. In a mixing bowl, combine the all-purpose flour, softened unsalted butter, granulated sugar, and a pinch of salt for the crust. Mix until the mixture resembles coarse crumbs.
3. Press the crust mixture evenly into the bottom of the prepared baking pan.
4. Bake the crust in the preheated oven for 15-20 minutes, or until lightly golden brown. Remove from the oven and set aside.
5. In a saucepan, combine the packed brown sugar, light corn syrup, and unsalted butter for the pecan filling. Cook over medium heat, stirring constantly, until the mixture comes to a boil.
6. Remove the saucepan from heat and let the mixture cool slightly.

7. In a small bowl, lightly beat the eggs with the vanilla extract. Gradually stir the beaten eggs into the slightly cooled brown sugar mixture, stirring constantly until well combined.
8. Fold in the pecan halves until they are evenly coated with the filling mixture.
9. Pour the pecan filling evenly over the partially baked crust in the baking pan.
10. Return the baking pan to the oven and bake for an additional 25-30 minutes, or until the filling is set and golden brown on top.
11. Remove from the oven and let the pecan pie bars cool completely in the pan on a wire rack.
12. Once cooled, use the parchment paper overhang to lift the pecan pie bars out of the pan and transfer them to a cutting board.
13. Cut the pecan pie bars into squares or rectangles.

MACADAMIA NUT COOKIES

- **Servings:** 24 cookies
- **Time:** 30 minutes

Ingredients:

- 1 cup unsalted butter, softened
- 1 cup granulated sugar
- 1 cup packed brown sugar
- 2 large eggs
- 1 teaspoon vanilla extract
- 2 1/2 cups all-purpose flour
- 1 teaspoon baking soda
- 1/2 teaspoon salt

- 1 1/2 cups macadamia nuts, chopped
- 1 cup white chocolate chips

Instructions:

1. Preheat your oven to 350°F (175°C). Line a baking sheet with parchment paper.
2. In a large mixing bowl, cream together the softened unsalted butter, granulated sugar, and packed brown sugar until light and fluffy.
3. Add the eggs, one at a time, beating well after each addition. Stir in the vanilla extract.
4. In a separate bowl, sift together the all-purpose flour, baking soda, and salt.
5. Gradually add the dry ingredients to the wet ingredients, mixing until well combined.
6. Fold in the chopped macadamia nuts and white chocolate chips until evenly distributed throughout the dough.
7. Drop rounded tablespoons of dough onto the prepared baking sheet, spacing them about 2 inches apart.
8. Bake in the preheated oven for 10-12 minutes, or until the edges are lightly golden brown.
9. Remove from the oven and let the cookies cool on the baking sheet for a few minutes before transferring them to a wire rack to cool completely.
10. Once cooled, store the macadamia nut cookies in an airtight container at room temperature for up to one week.

CASHEW VANILLA ICE CREAM

- **Servings:** About 6 servings

- **Time:** 6 hours (includes freezing time)

Ingredients:

- 2 cups raw cashews, soaked in water for 4-6 hours or overnight
- 1 (14 oz) can full-fat coconut milk
- 1/2 cup maple syrup or agave nectar
- 1 tablespoon vanilla extract
- Pinch of salt
- Optional: 1/2 cup chopped roasted cashews for garnish

Instructions:

1. Drain and rinse the soaked cashews under cold water.
2. In a blender, combine the soaked cashews, coconut milk, maple syrup or agave nectar, vanilla extract, and a pinch of salt.
3. Blend on high speed until the mixture is smooth and creamy, scraping down the sides of the blender as needed.
4. Transfer the cashew ice cream base into a shallow dish or ice cream maker container.
5. If using an ice cream maker, churn the mixture according to the manufacturer's instructions until it reaches a soft-serve consistency.
6. If not using an ice cream maker, cover the dish with plastic wrap and place it in the freezer. Every 30 minutes, remove the dish from the freezer and stir the mixture vigorously to break up any ice crystals. Repeat this process until the ice cream is firm and creamy, about 4-6 hours.
7. Once the ice cream is ready, scoop it into bowls or cones.

8. Optional: Sprinkle chopped roasted cashews over the top of each serving for added crunch and flavor.
9. Serve immediately for a soft-serve texture, or transfer any leftovers to an airtight container and store them in the freezer for later enjoyment.

DAIRY-FREE DELIGHTS

COCONUT FLOUR PANCAKES WITH BERRIES

- **Servings:** 4 servings
- **Time:** 20 minutes

Ingredients:

- 4 large eggs
- 1/2 cup coconut milk
- 2 tablespoons maple syrup or honey
- 1 teaspoon vanilla extract
- 1/2 cup coconut flour
- 1 teaspoon baking powder
- Pinch of salt
- Coconut oil or cooking spray, for greasing

- Fresh berries (such as strawberries, blueberries, raspberries) for serving
- Maple syrup or honey, for drizzling

Instructions:

1. In a mixing bowl, whisk together the eggs, coconut milk, maple syrup or honey, and vanilla extract until well combined.
2. In a separate bowl, sift together the coconut flour, baking powder, and a pinch of salt.
3. Gradually add the dry ingredients to the wet ingredients, stirring until a smooth batter forms. Let the batter sit for a few minutes to thicken.
4. Heat a non-stick skillet or griddle over medium heat. Lightly grease the skillet with coconut oil or cooking spray.
5. Pour about 1/4 cup of the pancake batter onto the skillet for each pancake, spreading it out slightly with the back of a spoon to form circles.
6. Cook the pancakes for 2-3 minutes, or until bubbles form on the surface and the edges look set.
7. Carefully flip the pancakes and cook for an additional 1-2 minutes on the other side, or until golden brown and cooked through.
8. Transfer the cooked pancakes to a plate and repeat with the remaining batter, greasing the skillet as needed.
9. Serve the coconut flour pancakes warm, topped with fresh berries and a drizzle of maple syrup or honey.

DAIRY-FREE VANILLA PUDDING

- **Servings:** 4 servings

- **Time:** 15 minutes (+ chilling time)

Ingredients:

- 2 cups unsweetened coconut milk (from a carton, not canned)
- 1/4 cup cornstarch
- 1/4 cup maple syrup or agave nectar
- 1 teaspoon vanilla extract
- Pinch of salt
- Fresh fruit or berries, for serving (optional)

Instructions:

1. In a medium saucepan, whisk together the coconut milk and cornstarch until smooth and well combined.
2. Place the saucepan over medium heat and bring the mixture to a simmer, stirring constantly.
3. Once the mixture begins to thicken, reduce the heat to low and continue to cook, stirring frequently, for 2-3 minutes or until it reaches a pudding-like consistency.
4. Remove the saucepan from the heat and stir in the maple syrup or agave nectar, vanilla extract, and a pinch of salt. Taste and adjust sweetness if needed.
5. Transfer the pudding to serving cups or ramekins.
6. Cover the pudding with plastic wrap, pressing it directly onto the surface of the pudding to prevent a skin from forming.
7. Chill the pudding in the refrigerator for at least 2-3 hours, or until completely chilled and set.
8. Once chilled, remove the plastic wrap and serve the dairy-free vanilla pudding with fresh fruit or berries if desired.

VEGAN CARROT CAKE CUPCAKES

- **Servings:** 12 cupcakes
- **Time:** 40 minutes

Ingredients:

For the Cupcakes:

- 1 1/2 cups all-purpose flour
- 1 teaspoon baking powder
- 1/2 teaspoon baking soda
- 1/4 teaspoon salt
- 1 teaspoon ground cinnamon
- 1/2 teaspoon ground nutmeg
- 1/2 cup coconut sugar or granulated sugar
- 1/4 cup maple syrup or agave nectar
- 1/2 cup unsweetened applesauce
- 1/4 cup coconut oil, melted
- 1 teaspoon vanilla extract
- 1 cup grated carrots
- 1/4 cup chopped walnuts or pecans (optional)
- 1/4 cup raisins (optional)

For the Vegan Cream Cheese Frosting:

- 1/2 cup vegan cream cheese, softened
- 1/4 cup vegan butter, softened
- 2 cups powdered sugar
- 1 teaspoon vanilla extract
- Zest of 1 lemon (optional)

Instructions:

1. Preheat your oven to 350°F (175°C). Line a muffin tin with paper liners.
2. In a large mixing bowl, sift together the all-purpose flour, baking powder, baking soda, salt, ground cinnamon, and ground nutmeg.
3. In another mixing bowl, whisk together the coconut sugar or granulated sugar, maple syrup or agave nectar, unsweetened applesauce, melted coconut oil, and vanilla extract until well combined.
4. Gradually add the wet ingredients to the dry ingredients, stirring until just combined.
5. Fold in the grated carrots, chopped nuts (if using), and raisins (if using) until evenly distributed throughout the batter.
6. Divide the batter evenly among the prepared muffin cups, filling each cup about 2/3 full.
7. Bake in the preheated oven for 18-20 minutes, or until a toothpick inserted into the center of a cupcake comes out clean.
8. Remove the cupcakes from the oven and let them cool in the muffin tin for a few minutes before transferring them to a wire rack to cool completely.
9. While the cupcakes are cooling, prepare the vegan cream cheese frosting. In a mixing bowl, beat together the vegan cream cheese and vegan butter until smooth and creamy.
10. Gradually add the powdered sugar, vanilla extract, and lemon zest (if using), beating until the frosting is smooth and fluffy.
11. Once the cupcakes are completely cool, frost them with the vegan cream cheese frosting.
12. Optionally, garnish each cupcake with a sprinkle of chopped nuts or a carrot decoration.

COCONUT MILK RICE PUDDING

- **Servings:** 4 servings
- **Time:** 1 hour

Ingredients:

- 1/2 cup white rice (such as jasmine or arborio)
- 1 (14 oz) can coconut milk
- 1/4 cup granulated sugar or coconut sugar
- 1 teaspoon vanilla extract
- Pinch of salt
- Optional toppings: toasted coconut flakes, chopped nuts, fresh fruit, cinnamon

Instructions:

1. Rinse the white rice under cold water until the water runs clear. Drain well.
2. In a medium saucepan, combine the rinsed rice, coconut milk, granulated sugar or coconut sugar, vanilla extract, and a pinch of salt.
3. Place the saucepan over medium heat and bring the mixture to a simmer, stirring occasionally.
4. Once the mixture begins to simmer, reduce the heat to low and let the rice cook, stirring occasionally, for 30-40 minutes or until the rice is tender and the mixture has thickened to a pudding-like consistency.
5. Taste the rice pudding and adjust sweetness if needed by adding more sugar.
6. Once the rice pudding is cooked to your desired consistency, remove the saucepan from the heat.

7. Serve the coconut milk rice pudding warm or chilled, topped with your favorite toppings such as toasted coconut flakes, chopped nuts, fresh fruit, or a sprinkle of cinnamon.

DAIRY-FREE CHOCOLATE ICE CREAM

- **Servings:** 6 servings
- **Time:** 6 hours (includes freezing time)

Ingredients:

- 2 (14 oz) cans full-fat coconut milk, chilled in the refrigerator overnight
- 1/2 cup cocoa powder
- 1/2 cup maple syrup or agave nectar
- 1 teaspoon vanilla extract
- Pinch of salt
- Optional: dairy-free chocolate chips, chopped nuts, or shredded coconut for topping

Instructions:

1. Chill the bowl of your ice cream maker in the freezer for at least 24 hours before making the ice cream.
2. In a mixing bowl, whisk together the cocoa powder, maple syrup or agave nectar, vanilla extract, and a pinch of salt until smooth and well combined.
3. Open the chilled cans of coconut milk and carefully scoop out the thick coconut cream that has solidified at the top of the cans, leaving behind the liquid coconut water (reserve this for another use, such as smoothies).

4. Place the coconut cream in a separate mixing bowl and beat it with a hand mixer or stand mixer until smooth and creamy.
5. Gradually add the cocoa mixture to the whipped coconut cream, beating until well combined and creamy.
6. Once the mixture is smooth and creamy, transfer it to the chilled bowl of your ice cream maker.
7. Churn the mixture according to the manufacturer's instructions until it reaches a soft-serve consistency.
8. If desired, fold in dairy-free chocolate chips, chopped nuts, or shredded coconut during the last few minutes of churning.
9. Transfer the churned ice cream to a freezer-safe container and smooth the top with a spatula.
10. Cover the container with a lid or plastic wrap, pressing it down onto the surface of the ice cream to prevent ice crystals from forming.
11. Freeze the ice cream for at least 4-6 hours, or until firm.
12. Once firm, scoop the dairy-free chocolate ice cream into bowls or cones, and serve.

VEGAN PUMPKIN PIE

- **Servings:** 8 servings
- **Time:** 1 hour 30 minutes (includes chilling time)

Ingredients:

For the Crust:

- 1 1/4 cups all-purpose flour
- 1/2 cup vegan butter, chilled and cubed
- 1/4 teaspoon salt

- 2-4 tablespoons ice water

For the Filling:

- 1 (15 oz) can pumpkin puree
- 3/4 cup full-fat coconut milk
- 1/2 cup maple syrup or agave nectar
- 1/4 cup cornstarch or arrowroot powder
- 2 teaspoons pumpkin pie spice
- 1 teaspoon vanilla extract
- 1/4 teaspoon salt

Instructions:

1. **Prepare the Crust:**
    - In a food processor, combine the all-purpose flour and salt. Add the chilled cubed vegan butter and pulse until the mixture resembles coarse crumbs.
    - Gradually add the ice water, 1 tablespoon at a time, and pulse until the dough comes together and forms a ball.
    - Flatten the dough into a disc, wrap it in plastic wrap, and refrigerate for at least 30 minutes.
2. **Preheat the Oven:**
    - Preheat your oven to 375°F (190°C).
3. **Roll Out the Crust:**
    - On a lightly floured surface, roll out the chilled dough into a circle large enough to fit into a 9-inch pie dish. Transfer the rolled-out dough to the pie dish and press it gently into the bottom and sides. Trim any excess dough and crimp the edges as desired.
4. **Prepare the Filling:**

- In a mixing bowl, whisk together the pumpkin puree, full-fat coconut milk, maple syrup or agave nectar, cornstarch or arrowroot powder, pumpkin pie spice, vanilla extract, and salt until smooth and well combined.

5. **Fill the Pie Crust:**
    - Pour the pumpkin filling into the prepared pie crust, smoothing the top with a spatula.
6. **Bake the Pie:**
    - Place the pie dish on a baking sheet and transfer it to the preheated oven.
    - Bake for 45-50 minutes, or until the filling is set and the crust is golden brown.
7. **Cool and Chill:**
    - Remove the pie from the oven and let it cool on a wire rack for at least 1 hour.
    - Once cooled, transfer the pie to the refrigerator and chill for at least 4 hours, or until fully set.
8. **Serve:**
    - Slice the chilled vegan pumpkin pie and serve it with dairy-free whipped cream or coconut whipped cream, if desired.

TOFU CHEESECAKE WITH BERRY COMPOTE

- **Servings:** 8 servings
- **Time:** 1 hour 30 minutes (includes chilling time)

Ingredients:

For the Crust:

- 1 1/2 cups graham cracker crumbs (or crushed vegan cookies)
- 1/4 cup vegan butter, melted

For the Cheesecake Filling:

- 1 (14 oz) block firm tofu, drained and pressed
- 1/2 cup raw cashews, soaked in water for 4-6 hours or overnight
- 1/3 cup maple syrup or agave nectar
- 1/4 cup coconut oil, melted
- 2 tablespoons lemon juice
- 1 teaspoon vanilla extract
- Pinch of salt

For the Berry Compote:

- 2 cups mixed berries (such as strawberries, blueberries, raspberries)
- 2 tablespoons maple syrup or agave nectar
- 1 tablespoon lemon juice
- 1 teaspoon cornstarch or arrowroot powder mixed with 1 tablespoon water (optional, for thickening)

Instructions:

1. **Prepare the Crust:**
    - Preheat your oven to 350°F (175°C). Grease a 9-inch springform pan.
    - In a mixing bowl, combine the graham cracker crumbs and melted vegan butter until well combined. Press the mixture into the bottom of the prepared springform pan. Bake for 8-10 minutes, then remove from the oven and let cool.

2. **Prepare the Cheesecake Filling:**
    - In a food processor or blender, combine the drained and pressed firm tofu, soaked raw cashews, maple syrup or agave nectar, melted coconut oil, lemon juice, vanilla extract, and a pinch of salt. Blend until smooth and creamy, scraping down the sides as needed.
3. **Assemble the Cheesecake:**
    - Pour the cheesecake filling over the cooled crust in the springform pan. Smooth the top with a spatula. Tap the pan gently on the counter to release any air bubbles.
4. **Bake the Cheesecake:**
    - Place the springform pan on a baking sheet and transfer it to the preheated oven. Bake for 45-50 minutes, or until the edges are set and the center is slightly jiggly.
5. **Cool and Chill:**
    - Remove the cheesecake from the oven and let it cool to room temperature. Once cooled, transfer it to the refrigerator and chill for at least 4 hours, or overnight, until fully set.
6. **Prepare the Berry Compote:**
    - In a saucepan, combine the mixed berries, maple syrup or agave nectar, and lemon juice. Cook over medium heat until the berries start to break down and release their juices, stirring occasionally.
    - If desired, thicken the compote by adding the cornstarch or arrowroot powder mixed with water. Cook for an additional 1-2 minutes, or until thickened. Remove from heat and let cool.
7. **Serve:**

- Once the cheesecake is fully chilled and set, remove it from the refrigerator. Run a knife around the edges of the springform pan to loosen the cheesecake, then release the sides of the pan.
- Serve slices of the tofu cheesecake topped with the berry compote.

AVOCADO LIME TART

- **Servings:** 8 servings
- **Time:** 1 hour 30 minutes (includes chilling time)

Ingredients:

For the Crust:

- 1 1/2 cups almond flour
- 1/4 cup coconut oil, melted
- 2 tablespoons maple syrup or agave nectar
- Pinch of salt

For the Filling:

- 2 ripe avocados
- 1/2 cup full-fat coconut milk
- 1/2 cup maple syrup or agave nectar
- Zest and juice of 2 limes
- 1 teaspoon vanilla extract
- Pinch of salt

For Garnish (optional):

- Lime slices

- Lime zest
- Whipped coconut cream

Instructions:

1. **Prepare the Crust:**
    - Preheat your oven to 350°F (175°C). Grease a 9-inch tart pan with a removable bottom.
    - In a mixing bowl, combine the almond flour, melted coconut oil, maple syrup or agave nectar, and a pinch of salt. Stir until the mixture resembles coarse crumbs.
    - Press the crust mixture evenly into the bottom and up the sides of the prepared tart pan.
    - Bake the crust in the preheated oven for 10-12 minutes, or until golden brown. Remove from the oven and let it cool completely.
2. **Prepare the Filling:**
    - In a food processor or blender, combine the ripe avocados, full-fat coconut milk, maple syrup or agave nectar, lime zest and juice, vanilla extract, and a pinch of salt. Blend until smooth and creamy, scraping down the sides as needed.
3. **Assemble the Tart:**
    - Pour the avocado lime filling into the cooled tart crust, smoothing the top with a spatula.
4. **Chill the Tart:**
    - Place the tart in the refrigerator and chill for at least 1 hour, or until the filling is set.
5. **Garnish (optional):**
    - Before serving, garnish the tart with lime slices, lime zest, and whipped coconut cream, if desired.

- Slice the chilled avocado lime tart into wedges and serve.

DAIRY-FREE BANANA BREAD

- **Servings:** 10 slices
- **Time:** 1 hour 15 minutes

Ingredients:

- 2 cups all-purpose flour
- 1 teaspoon baking powder
- 1/2 teaspoon baking soda
- 1/2 teaspoon salt
- 1 teaspoon ground cinnamon
- 1/4 teaspoon ground nutmeg
- 3 ripe bananas, mashed
- 1/2 cup coconut sugar or granulated sugar
- 1/3 cup coconut oil, melted
- 1/4 cup unsweetened applesauce
- 1 teaspoon vanilla extract
- Optional mix-ins: chopped nuts, chocolate chips, or dried fruit

Instructions:

1. **Preheat the Oven:**
   - Preheat your oven to 350°F (175°C). Grease a 9x5-inch loaf pan or line it with parchment paper.
2. **Prepare the Dry Ingredients:**
   - In a large mixing bowl, whisk together the all-purpose flour, baking powder, baking soda, salt,

ground cinnamon, and ground nutmeg until well combined.

3. **Prepare the Wet Ingredients:**
   - In a separate mixing bowl, combine the mashed bananas, coconut sugar or granulated sugar, melted coconut oil, unsweetened applesauce, and vanilla extract. Mix until smooth and well combined.

4. **Combine Wet and Dry Ingredients:**
   - Pour the wet ingredients into the bowl with the dry ingredients. Stir until just combined. Be careful not to overmix; a few lumps are okay.
   - If using any optional mix-ins such as chopped nuts, chocolate chips, or dried fruit, gently fold them into the batter.

5. **Bake the Banana Bread:**
   - Pour the batter into the prepared loaf pan, spreading it out evenly.
   - Bake in the preheated oven for 55-65 minutes, or until a toothpick inserted into the center of the bread comes out clean.
   - If the top of the bread starts to brown too quickly, you can loosely cover it with aluminum foil during the last 15-20 minutes of baking to prevent over-browning.

6. **Cool and Serve:**
   - Once baked, remove the banana bread from the oven and let it cool in the pan for about 10 minutes.
   - Transfer the banana bread to a wire rack to cool completely before slicing and serving.

VEGAN CHOCOLATE MOUSSE PIE

- **Servings:** 8 servings
- **Time:** 4 hours 30 minutes (includes chilling time)

Ingredients:

For the Crust:

- 1 1/2 cups chocolate cookie crumbs (use vegan cookies)
- 1/4 cup vegan butter, melted

For the Chocolate Mousse Filling:

- 2 ripe avocados
- 1/2 cup cocoa powder
- 1/2 cup maple syrup or agave nectar
- 1/4 cup full-fat coconut milk
- 1 teaspoon vanilla extract
- Pinch of salt

For Garnish (optional):

- Vegan whipped cream
- Chocolate shavings
- Fresh berries

Instructions:

1. **Prepare the Crust:**
    - Preheat your oven to 350°F (175°C). Grease a 9-inch pie dish.

- In a mixing bowl, combine the chocolate cookie crumbs and melted vegan butter until well combined.
 - Press the mixture into the bottom and up the sides of the prepared pie dish to form the crust.
 - Bake the crust in the preheated oven for 8-10 minutes. Remove from the oven and let it cool completely.
2. **Prepare the Chocolate Mousse Filling:**
 - In a food processor or blender, combine the ripe avocados, cocoa powder, maple syrup or agave nectar, full-fat coconut milk, vanilla extract, and a pinch of salt.
 - Blend until smooth and creamy, scraping down the sides as needed. Taste and adjust sweetness if necessary.
3. **Assemble the Pie:**
 - Pour the chocolate mousse filling into the cooled crust, spreading it out evenly with a spatula.
4. **Chill the Pie:**
 - Place the pie in the refrigerator and chill for at least 4 hours, or until the filling is set.
5. **Garnish (optional):**
 - Before serving, garnish the pie with dollops of vegan whipped cream, chocolate shavings, and fresh berries, if desired.
 - Slice the chilled vegan chocolate mousse pie and serve.

LOW-CARB CREATIONS

KETO LEMON CHEESECAKE BITES

- **Servings:** 12 bites
- **Time:** 2 hours 30 minutes (includes chilling time)

Ingredients:

For the Crust:

- 1 cup almond flour
- 2 tablespoons coconut oil, melted
- 1 tablespoon powdered erythritol or sweetener of choice
- Zest of 1 lemon

For the Cheesecake Filling:

- 8 oz cream cheese, softened

- 1/4 cup powdered erythritol or sweetener of choice
- 2 tablespoons lemon juice
- Zest of 1 lemon
- 1 teaspoon vanilla extract

Instructions:

1. **Prepare the Crust:**
    - In a mixing bowl, combine the almond flour, melted coconut oil, powdered erythritol, and lemon zest until well combined.
    - Press the mixture firmly into the bottom of a lined 8x8-inch baking dish or similar-sized container.
    - Place the crust in the refrigerator to chill while you prepare the filling.
2. **Prepare the Cheesecake Filling:**
    - In a mixing bowl, beat the softened cream cheese until smooth and creamy.
    - Add the powdered erythritol, lemon juice, lemon zest, and vanilla extract. Beat until well combined and smooth.
3. **Assemble the Cheesecake Bites:**
    - Remove the chilled crust from the refrigerator.
    - Spread the cheesecake filling evenly over the crust in the baking dish.
4. **Chill the Cheesecake Bites:**
    - Cover the baking dish with plastic wrap and place it in the refrigerator to chill for at least 2 hours, or until firm.
5. **Slice into Bites:**
    - Once the cheesecake is firm, remove it from the refrigerator and lift it out of the baking dish using the parchment paper.

- Use a sharp knife to slice the cheesecake into 12 equal-sized squares or bites.
6. **Serve:**
    - Serve the keto lemon cheesecake bites chilled.
    - Optionally, garnish with additional lemon zest or a small dollop of whipped cream before serving.

LOW-CARB BLUEBERRY MUFFINS

- **Servings:** 12 muffins
- **Time:** 30 minutes

Ingredients:

- 2 cups almond flour
- 1/4 cup coconut flour
- 1/3 cup powdered erythritol or sweetener of choice
- 1 teaspoon baking powder
- 1/2 teaspoon baking soda
- Pinch of salt
- 3 large eggs
- 1/2 cup unsweetened almond milk or coconut milk
- 1/4 cup melted coconut oil or butter
- 1 teaspoon vanilla extract
- 1 cup fresh or frozen blueberries

Instructions:

1. **Preheat the Oven:**
    - Preheat your oven to 350°F (175°C). Line a muffin tin with paper liners or grease it with coconut oil.
2. **Prepare the Dry Ingredients:**

- In a large mixing bowl, whisk together the almond flour, coconut flour, powdered erythritol, baking powder, baking soda, and salt until well combined.
3. **Prepare the Wet Ingredients:**
    - In a separate mixing bowl, beat the eggs. Add the almond milk, melted coconut oil or butter, and vanilla extract. Mix until well combined.
4. **Combine Wet and Dry Ingredients:**
    - Gradually add the wet ingredients to the dry ingredients, stirring until just combined. Be careful not to overmix.
    - Gently fold in the blueberries until evenly distributed throughout the batter.
5. **Fill the Muffin Cups:**
    - Spoon the batter into the prepared muffin cups, filling each cup about 3/4 full.
6. **Bake the Muffins:**
    - Place the muffin tin in the preheated oven and bake for 20-25 minutes, or until the muffins are golden brown and a toothpick inserted into the center comes out clean.
7. **Cool and Serve:**
    - Remove the muffin tin from the oven and let the muffins cool in the tin for a few minutes before transferring them to a wire rack to cool completely.

SUGAR-FREE COCONUT CREAM PIE

- **Servings:** 8 slices
- **Time:** 4 hours 30 minutes (includes chilling time)

Ingredients:

For the Crust:

- 1 1/2 cups almond flour
- 1/4 cup coconut oil, melted
- 2 tablespoons powdered erythritol or sweetener of choice
- Pinch of salt

For the Coconut Cream Filling:

- 1 (14 oz) can full-fat coconut milk
- 1/4 cup powdered erythritol or sweetener of choice
- 1/4 cup coconut flour
- 3 large egg yolks
- 1 teaspoon vanilla extract
- 1 cup unsweetened shredded coconut

For the Topping:

- 1 cup heavy cream or coconut cream, chilled
- 1 tablespoon powdered erythritol or sweetener of choice
- Unsweetened shredded coconut, toasted (optional, for garnish)

Instructions:

1. **Prepare the Crust:**
    - Preheat your oven to 350°F (175°C). Grease a 9-inch pie dish.
    - In a mixing bowl, combine the almond flour, melted coconut oil, powdered erythritol, and a pinch of salt until well combined.

- Press the mixture firmly into the bottom and up the sides of the prepared pie dish to form the crust.
- Bake the crust in the preheated oven for 10-12 minutes, or until golden brown. Remove from the oven and let it cool completely.

2. **Prepare the Coconut Cream Filling:**
   - In a saucepan, whisk together the full-fat coconut milk, powdered erythritol, and coconut flour over medium heat.
   - Cook, stirring constantly, until the mixture thickens, about 5-7 minutes.
   - In a separate mixing bowl, whisk the egg yolks. Gradually whisk in a small amount of the hot coconut milk mixture to temper the eggs.
   - Pour the egg mixture back into the saucepan with the remaining coconut milk mixture. Cook, stirring constantly, for an additional 2-3 minutes, or until thickened.
   - Remove the saucepan from the heat and stir in the vanilla extract and unsweetened shredded coconut.
   - Let the filling cool slightly, then pour it into the cooled pie crust. Smooth the top with a spatula.

3. **Chill the Pie:**
   - Cover the pie with plastic wrap, pressing it directly onto the surface of the filling to prevent a skin from forming.
   - Place the pie in the refrigerator to chill for at least 4 hours, or until set.

4. **Prepare the Topping:**

- In a mixing bowl, beat the chilled heavy cream or coconut cream with powdered erythritol until stiff peaks form.
- Spread the whipped cream over the chilled coconut cream pie.
5. **Garnish and Serve:**
    - Optionally, garnish the pie with toasted unsweetened shredded coconut before serving.

AVOCADO CHOCOLATE PUDDING

- **Servings:** 4 servings
- **Time:** 10 minutes

Ingredients:

- 2 ripe avocados
- 1/4 cup unsweetened cocoa powder
- 1/4 cup maple syrup or agave nectar
- 1/4 cup almond milk or coconut milk
- 1 teaspoon vanilla extract
- Pinch of salt
- Optional toppings: sliced strawberries, raspberries, or shaved dark chocolate

Instructions:

1. **Prepare the Avocados:**
    - Cut the avocados in half and remove the pits. Scoop the flesh into a food processor or blender.
2. **Blend the Ingredients:**
    - Add the unsweetened cocoa powder, maple syrup or agave nectar, almond milk or coconut milk,

vanilla extract, and a pinch of salt to the food processor or blender with the avocado.
- Blend until smooth and creamy, scraping down the sides as needed. Taste and adjust sweetness if necessary by adding more maple syrup or agave nectar.

3. **Chill (optional):**
    - If you prefer your pudding chilled, transfer it to a bowl or individual serving cups and refrigerate for 1-2 hours before serving. This will also allow the flavors to meld together.

4. **Serve:**
    - Once chilled (if desired), divide the avocado chocolate pudding among serving cups.
    - Optionally, garnish each serving with sliced strawberries, raspberries, or shaved dark chocolate.

LOW-CARB CHEESECAKE BROWNIES

- **Servings:** 16 brownies
- **Time:** 1 hour 30 minutes

Ingredients:

For the Brownie Layer:

- 1/2 cup unsweetened cocoa powder
- 1/2 cup almond flour
- 1/4 cup coconut flour
- 1/2 cup powdered erythritol or sweetener of choice
- 1/2 teaspoon baking powder
- 1/4 teaspoon salt

- 1/2 cup unsalted butter, melted
- 3 large eggs
- 1 teaspoon vanilla extract

For the Cheesecake Layer:

- 8 oz cream cheese, softened
- 1/4 cup powdered erythritol or sweetener of choice
- 1 large egg
- 1 teaspoon vanilla extract

Instructions:

1. **Preheat the Oven:**
   - Preheat your oven to 350°F (175°C). Grease or line an 8x8-inch baking dish with parchment paper.
2. **Prepare the Brownie Batter:**
   - In a mixing bowl, whisk together the unsweetened cocoa powder, almond flour, coconut flour, powdered erythritol, baking powder, and salt until well combined.
   - Add the melted butter, eggs, and vanilla extract to the dry ingredients. Mix until smooth and well combined.
3. **Prepare the Cheesecake Batter:**
   - In a separate mixing bowl, beat the softened cream cheese until smooth and creamy.
   - Add the powdered erythritol, egg, and vanilla extract to the cream cheese. Beat until smooth and well combined.
4. **Assemble the Brownies:**
   - Spread half of the brownie batter evenly into the bottom of the prepared baking dish.

- Pour the cheesecake batter over the brownie batter and spread it out evenly with a spatula.
- Dollop the remaining brownie batter over the cheesecake layer.
- Use a knife to gently swirl the batters together to create a marbled effect.

5. **Bake the Brownies:**
    - Place the baking dish in the preheated oven and bake for 25-30 minutes, or until the edges are set and the center is slightly jiggly.

6. **Cool and Slice:**
    - Remove the brownies from the oven and let them cool completely in the baking dish on a wire rack.
    - Once cooled, transfer the brownies to the refrigerator and chill for at least 1 hour before slicing into squares.
    - Slice the chilled low-carb cheesecake brownies into squares and serve.

KETO-FRIENDLY CHOCOLATE CHIP COOKIES

- **Servings:** 16 cookies
- **Time:** 25 minutes

Ingredients:

- 1 1/2 cups almond flour
- 1/4 cup coconut flour
- 1/2 teaspoon baking soda
- 1/4 teaspoon salt
- 1/3 cup coconut oil, melted

- 1/3 cup powdered erythritol or sweetener of choice
- 1 large egg
- 1 teaspoon vanilla extract
- 1/2 cup sugar-free chocolate chips

Instructions:

1. **Preheat the Oven:**
    - Preheat your oven to 350°F (175°C). Line a baking sheet with parchment paper or silicone baking mats.
2. **Prepare the Dry Ingredients:**
    - In a mixing bowl, whisk together the almond flour, coconut flour, baking soda, and salt until well combined.
3. **Prepare the Wet Ingredients:**
    - In a separate mixing bowl, beat together the melted coconut oil and powdered erythritol until smooth.
    - Add the egg and vanilla extract to the coconut oil mixture and beat until well combined.
4. **Combine Wet and Dry Ingredients:**
    - Gradually add the dry ingredients to the wet ingredients, stirring until a dough forms.
    - Fold in the sugar-free chocolate chips until evenly distributed throughout the dough.
5. **Shape the Cookies:**
    - Use a cookie scoop or spoon to portion out the dough and roll it into balls.
    - Place the cookie dough balls onto the prepared baking sheet, spacing them about 2 inches apart.
6. **Flatten the Cookies:**

- Use the palm of your hand or the bottom of a glass to gently flatten each cookie dough ball into a disk shape.
7. **Bake the Cookies:**
    - Place the baking sheet in the preheated oven and bake for 10-12 minutes, or until the edges of the cookies are golden brown.
8. **Cool and Serve:**
    - Remove the cookies from the oven and let them cool on the baking sheet for 5 minutes before transferring them to a wire rack to cool completely.

ALMOND FLOUR ZUCCHINI BREAD

- **Servings:** 10 slices
- **Time:** 1 hour 15 minutes

Ingredients:

- 2 cups almond flour
- 1 teaspoon baking powder
- 1/2 teaspoon baking soda
- 1/2 teaspoon salt
- 1 teaspoon ground cinnamon
- 3 large eggs
- 1/4 cup coconut oil, melted
- 1/3 cup honey or maple syrup
- 1 teaspoon vanilla extract
- 1 1/2 cups grated zucchini (about 1 medium zucchini)
- Optional add-ins: chopped nuts, chocolate chips, or raisins

Instructions:

1. **Preheat the Oven:**
   - Preheat your oven to 350°F (175°C). Grease or line a 9x5-inch loaf pan with parchment paper.
2. **Prepare the Dry Ingredients:**
   - In a large mixing bowl, whisk together the almond flour, baking powder, baking soda, salt, and ground cinnamon until well combined.
3. **Prepare the Wet Ingredients:**
   - In a separate mixing bowl, whisk together the eggs, melted coconut oil, honey or maple syrup, and vanilla extract until smooth.
4. **Combine Wet and Dry Ingredients:**
   - Gradually add the wet ingredients to the dry ingredients, stirring until just combined.
   - Fold in the grated zucchini and any optional add-ins until evenly distributed throughout the batter.
5. **Bake the Bread:**
   - Pour the batter into the prepared loaf pan and smooth the top with a spatula.
   - Place the loaf pan in the preheated oven and bake for 45-55 minutes, or until a toothpick inserted into the center comes out clean.
6. **Cool and Serve:**
   - Remove the zucchini bread from the oven and let it cool in the loaf pan for 10 minutes.
   - Carefully transfer the bread to a wire rack to cool completely before slicing.

PUMPKIN SPICE CHIA PUDDING

- **Servings:** 4 servings
- **Time:** 4 hours 10 minutes (includes chilling time)

Ingredients:

- 1 cup unsweetened almond milk or coconut milk
- 1/2 cup canned pumpkin puree
- 1/4 cup chia seeds
- 2 tablespoons maple syrup or honey (optional, adjust to taste)
- 1 teaspoon vanilla extract
- 1 teaspoon pumpkin pie spice
- Optional toppings: chopped nuts, pumpkin seeds, whipped coconut cream, or a sprinkle of cinnamon

Instructions:

1. **Mix Ingredients:**
   - In a mixing bowl or large jar, combine the almond milk or coconut milk, canned pumpkin puree, chia seeds, maple syrup or honey (if using), vanilla extract, and pumpkin pie spice. Stir well to combine.
2. **Chill Mixture:**
   - Cover the bowl or jar and refrigerate the mixture for at least 4 hours, or preferably overnight, to allow the chia seeds to thicken and absorb the liquid.
3. **Stir Before Serving:**
   - Before serving, give the pumpkin spice chia pudding a good stir to ensure that the ingredients are well mixed and evenly distributed.
4. **Serve:**

- Divide the chilled pumpkin spice chia pudding among serving bowls or glasses.
5. **Top and Enjoy:**
    - Optionally, top each serving with chopped nuts, pumpkin seeds, whipped coconut cream, or a sprinkle of cinnamon for extra flavor and texture.

LOW-CARB STRAWBERRY SHORTCAKE

- **Servings:** 6 servings
- **Time:** 30 minutes

Ingredients:

For the Shortcakes:

- 2 cups almond flour
- 1/4 cup coconut flour
- 1/4 cup powdered erythritol or sweetener of choice
- 1 tablespoon baking powder
- 1/4 teaspoon salt
- 1/2 cup unsalted butter, cold and cubed
- 3 large eggs
- 1 teaspoon vanilla extract

For the Strawberry Filling:

- 2 cups fresh strawberries, sliced
- 2 tablespoons powdered erythritol or sweetener of choice
- 1 teaspoon lemon juice

For the Whipped Cream:

- 1 cup heavy cream or coconut cream, chilled
- 1 tablespoon powdered erythritol or sweetener of choice
- 1 teaspoon vanilla extract

Instructions:

1. **Preheat the Oven:**
   - Preheat your oven to 350°F (175°C). Line a baking sheet with parchment paper.
2. **Prepare the Shortcakes:**
   - In a large mixing bowl, whisk together the almond flour, coconut flour, powdered erythritol, baking powder, and salt.
   - Add the cold, cubed butter to the dry ingredients. Use a pastry cutter or fork to cut the butter into the flour mixture until it resembles coarse crumbs.
   - In a separate bowl, whisk together the eggs and vanilla extract. Pour the wet ingredients into the dry ingredients and stir until a dough forms.
3. **Shape the Shortcakes:**
   - Divide the dough into 6 equal portions. Shape each portion into a round disk and place it on the prepared baking sheet, spacing them evenly apart.
4. **Bake the Shortcakes:**
   - Bake in the preheated oven for 15-18 minutes, or until the shortcakes are golden brown and cooked through.
   - Remove from the oven and let them cool on the baking sheet for a few minutes before transferring them to a wire rack to cool completely.
5. **Prepare the Strawberry Filling:**
   - In a mixing bowl, combine the sliced strawberries, powdered erythritol, and lemon juice. Stir well to

coat the strawberries in the sweetener. Let them macerate for a few minutes to release their juices.
6. **Prepare the Whipped Cream:**
    - In a mixing bowl, beat the chilled heavy cream or coconut cream with powdered erythritol and vanilla extract until stiff peaks form.
7. **Assemble the Shortcakes:**
    - To serve, slice each shortcake in half horizontally. Place the bottom half on a serving plate.
    - Spoon some of the macerated strawberries onto the bottom half of each shortcake. Top with a dollop of whipped cream.
    - Place the top half of the shortcake on top of the whipped cream. Repeat with the remaining shortcakes.
8. **Serve:**
    - Serve the low-carb strawberry shortcakes immediately, garnished with additional whipped cream and strawberries if desired.

SUGAR-FREE CHEESECAKE WITH RASPBERRY SAUCE

- **Servings:** 8 servings
- **Time:** 4 hours 30 minutes (includes chilling time)

Ingredients:

For the Cheesecake:

- 16 oz cream cheese, softened
- 1/2 cup powdered erythritol or sweetener of choice
- 2 large eggs

- 1 teaspoon vanilla extract
- 1/4 cup sour cream or Greek yogurt
- 1 tablespoon lemon juice
- Zest of 1 lemon

For the Raspberry Sauce:

- 1 1/2 cups fresh or frozen raspberries
- 2 tablespoons powdered erythritol or sweetener of choice
- 1 tablespoon lemon juice
- 1 tablespoon water

Instructions:

1. **Preheat the Oven:**
   - Preheat your oven to 325°F (160°C). Grease a 9-inch springform pan with coconut oil or line it with parchment paper.
2. **Prepare the Cheesecake Batter:**
   - In a large mixing bowl, beat the softened cream cheese and powdered erythritol until smooth and creamy.
   - Add the eggs, one at a time, beating well after each addition.
   - Stir in the vanilla extract, sour cream or Greek yogurt, lemon juice, and lemon zest until well combined and smooth.
3. **Bake the Cheesecake:**
   - Pour the cheesecake batter into the prepared springform pan and spread it out evenly with a spatula.

- Place the pan in the preheated oven and bake for 40-45 minutes, or until the edges are set and the center is slightly jiggly.
- Turn off the oven and leave the cheesecake inside with the door closed for an additional 10 minutes.
- Remove the cheesecake from the oven and let it cool completely on a wire rack.

4. **Prepare the Raspberry Sauce:**
   - In a small saucepan, combine the raspberries, powdered erythritol, lemon juice, and water.
   - Bring the mixture to a simmer over medium heat, stirring occasionally.
   - Cook for 5-7 minutes, or until the raspberries have broken down and the sauce has thickened slightly.
   - Remove the saucepan from the heat and let the raspberry sauce cool to room temperature.

5. **Chill the Cheesecake:**
   - Once cooled to room temperature, refrigerate the cheesecake for at least 4 hours, or preferably overnight, to set.

6. **Serve:**
   - When ready to serve, release the cheesecake from the springform pan and transfer it to a serving plate.
   - Slice the cheesecake into portions and serve each slice with a drizzle of raspberry sauce.

INTERNATIONAL FLAVORS

GREEK YOGURT HONEY BAKLAVA BITES

- **Servings:** 12 bites
- **Time:** 30 minutes

Ingredients:

- 1 cup Greek yogurt
- 2 tablespoons honey
- 1/4 teaspoon ground cinnamon
- 1/4 cup chopped walnuts
- 1/4 cup chopped pistachios
- 1/4 cup honey, for drizzling
- 6 sheets phyllo dough
- Cooking spray or melted butter

Instructions:

1. **Preheat the Oven:**
   - Preheat your oven to 350°F (175°C).
2. **Prepare the Yogurt Filling:**
   - In a mixing bowl, combine the Greek yogurt, 2 tablespoons of honey, and ground cinnamon. Mix until well combined. Set aside.
3. **Prepare the Nut Mixture:**
   - In another bowl, mix together the chopped walnuts and chopped pistachios. Set aside.
4. **Assemble the Baklava Bites:**
   - Lay one sheet of phyllo dough flat on a clean surface. Lightly coat it with cooking spray or brush it with melted butter.
   - Place another sheet of phyllo dough on top and repeat the process until you have a stack of 3 sheets.
   - Cut the stacked phyllo dough into 12 equal squares.
5. **Fill and Fold the Bites:**
   - Place a spoonful of the Greek yogurt mixture in the center of each phyllo square.
   - Top each with a sprinkle of the nut mixture.
   - Fold the corners of each phyllo square over the filling to form a little packet or triangle.
6. **Bake the Bites:**
   - Place the filled baklava bites on a baking sheet lined with parchment paper.
   - Bake in the preheated oven for 10-12 minutes, or until the phyllo dough is golden brown and crispy.
7. **Drizzle with Honey:**

- o Remove the baklava bites from the oven and let them cool slightly.
- o Drizzle each bite with a little honey before serving.

JAPANESE MATCHA GREEN TEA POPSICLES

- **Servings:** 6 popsicles
- **Time:** 6 hours (includes freezing time)

Ingredients:

- 2 teaspoons matcha green tea powder
- 2 tablespoons hot water
- 1 1/2 cups coconut milk
- 1/4 cup honey or maple syrup (adjust to taste)
- 1 teaspoon vanilla extract
- Optional: sweetened condensed milk or condensed coconut milk for extra creaminess (adjust to taste)

Instructions:

1. **Prepare the Matcha Mixture:**
    - o In a small bowl, whisk together the matcha green tea powder and hot water until smooth. Set aside to cool.
2. **Mix the Popsicle Base:**
    - o In a mixing bowl, combine the coconut milk, honey or maple syrup, and vanilla extract. Stir until well combined.
    - o If using, add sweetened condensed milk or condensed coconut milk for extra creaminess, adjusting the sweetness to taste.

3. **Combine Matcha and Popsicle Base:**
   - Gradually add the prepared matcha mixture to the coconut milk mixture, stirring until evenly distributed and the color is uniform.
4. **Pour into Popsicle Molds:**
   - Pour the matcha coconut milk mixture into popsicle molds, filling each mold to the top.
   - Insert popsicle sticks into each mold.
5. **Freeze:**
   - Place the popsicle molds in the freezer and freeze for at least 6 hours, or until the popsicles are completely set.
6. **Unmold and Serve:**
   - Once the popsicles are frozen solid, remove them from the molds by running warm water over the outside of the molds for a few seconds.
   - Gently pull the popsicles out of the molds and serve immediately.

INDIAN MANGO LASSI SMOOTHIE

- **Servings:** 2 smoothies
- **Time:** 10 minutes

Ingredients:

- 1 cup ripe mango chunks, fresh or frozen
- 1/2 cup plain Greek yogurt
- 1/2 cup milk (dairy or non-dairy)
- 2 tablespoons honey or maple syrup (adjust to taste)
- 1/4 teaspoon ground cardamom (optional)
- Ice cubes (optional, if using fresh mango)

Instructions:

1. **Prepare the Ingredients:**
   - If using fresh mango, peel and chop the mango into chunks. If using frozen mango, ensure it is thawed before use.
2. **Blend the Ingredients:**
   - In a blender, combine the mango chunks, plain Greek yogurt, milk, honey or maple syrup, and ground cardamom (if using).
   - If using fresh mango and desire a colder smoothie, add a handful of ice cubes to the blender as well.
3. **Blend Until Smooth:**
   - Blend the ingredients on high speed until smooth and creamy. If the smoothie is too thick, you can add a little more milk to reach your desired consistency.
4. **Taste and Adjust:**
   - Taste the smoothie and adjust the sweetness by adding more honey or maple syrup if desired.
5. **Serve:**
   - Pour the mango lassi smoothie into glasses.
   - Optionally, garnish with a sprinkle of ground cardamom or a few mango chunks on top for presentation.

ITALIAN AFFOGATO WITH SUGAR-FREE ESPRESSO

- **Servings:** 1
- **Time:** 5 minutes

Ingredients:

- 1 shot (about 1 ounce) sugar-free espresso or strongly brewed coffee
- 1 scoop sugar-free vanilla ice cream or gelato
- Optional: sugar-free chocolate shavings or cocoa powder for garnish

Instructions:

1. **Prepare the Espresso:**
    - Brew a shot of sugar-free espresso using an espresso machine or a moka pot. Alternatively, prepare a strong cup of sugar-free coffee using your preferred brewing method.
2. **Scoop the Ice Cream:**
    - Place a scoop of sugar-free vanilla ice cream or gelato into a serving glass or cup.
3. **Pour the Espresso:**
    - Pour the hot sugar-free espresso directly over the scoop of ice cream. The heat from the espresso will begin to melt the ice cream, creating a delicious blend of flavors and textures.
4. **Garnish (Optional):**
    - Optionally, garnish the affogato with sugar-free chocolate shavings or a sprinkle of cocoa powder for an extra touch of indulgence.
5. **Serve Immediately:**
    - Serve the Italian affogato immediately while the espresso is hot and the ice cream is melting.

MEXICAN SPICED CHOCOLATE AVOCADO MOUSSE

- **Servings:** 4
- **Time:** 10 minutes

Ingredients:

- 2 ripe avocados
- 1/4 cup unsweetened cocoa powder
- 1/4 cup honey or maple syrup
- 1 teaspoon vanilla extract
- 1/2 teaspoon ground cinnamon
- 1/4 teaspoon ground nutmeg
- Pinch of chili powder (adjust to taste)
- Pinch of salt
- Optional toppings: whipped coconut cream, sliced strawberries, or shaved dark chocolate

Instructions:

1. **Prepare the Avocados:**
   - Cut the avocados in half, remove the pits, and scoop the flesh into a blender or food processor.
2. **Blend the Ingredients:**
   - Add the unsweetened cocoa powder, honey or maple syrup, vanilla extract, ground cinnamon, ground nutmeg, chili powder, and a pinch of salt to the blender or food processor with the avocado.
   - Blend until smooth and creamy, scraping down the sides as needed. Taste and adjust sweetness or spice levels if necessary.
3. **Chill (Optional):**

- If you prefer a chilled mousse, transfer it to a bowl or individual serving cups and refrigerate for 1-2 hours before serving. This will also allow the flavors to meld together.
4. **Serve:**
    - Once chilled (if desired), divide the chocolate avocado mousse among serving cups.
5. **Garnish (Optional):**
    - Top each serving with a dollop of whipped coconut cream, sliced strawberries, or shaved dark chocolate for extra flavor and texture.

FRENCH RASPBERRY CLAFOUTIS

- **Servings:** 6
- **Time:** 50 minutes

Ingredients:

- 1 cup fresh raspberries
- 3 large eggs
- 1/2 cup granulated sugar
- 1 cup whole milk
- 1/2 cup all-purpose flour
- 1 teaspoon vanilla extract
- Pinch of salt
- Powdered sugar, for dusting (optional)
- Whipped cream or vanilla ice cream, for serving (optional)

Instructions:

1. **Preheat the Oven:**

- Preheat your oven to 350°F (175°C). Grease a 9-inch round baking dish with butter or cooking spray.
2. **Prepare the Raspberries:**
    - Rinse the fresh raspberries under cold water and pat them dry with a paper towel. Arrange the raspberries in a single layer in the greased baking dish.
3. **Make the Batter:**
    - In a mixing bowl, whisk together the eggs and granulated sugar until pale and slightly thickened.
    - Gradually whisk in the milk, then add the flour, vanilla extract, and a pinch of salt. Whisk until smooth and well combined.
4. **Assemble the Clafoutis:**
    - Pour the batter over the raspberries in the baking dish, ensuring that the raspberries are evenly distributed.
5. **Bake:**
    - Place the baking dish in the preheated oven and bake for 35-40 minutes, or until the clafoutis is puffed and golden brown on top, and a toothpick inserted into the center comes out clean.
6. **Cool:**
    - Remove the clafoutis from the oven and let it cool slightly before serving. The clafoutis will deflate slightly as it cools.
7. **Serve:**
    - Dust the top of the clafoutis with powdered sugar, if desired.
    - Slice the clafoutis into wedges and serve warm or at room temperature.

- Optionally, serve with whipped cream or vanilla ice cream on the side.

THAI COCONUT MANGO STICKY RICE

- **Servings:** 4
- **Time:** 1 hour (plus soaking time)

Ingredients:

- 1 cup glutinous rice (also known as sticky rice or sweet rice)
- 1 cup coconut milk
- 1/4 cup granulated sugar
- 1/4 teaspoon salt
- 2 ripe mangoes, peeled and sliced
- Toasted sesame seeds or shredded coconut, for garnish (optional)

Instructions:

1. **Prepare the Rice:**
    - Rinse the glutinous rice under cold water until the water runs clear. Then, soak the rice in water for at least 4 hours or overnight.
2. **Steam the Rice:**
    - Drain the soaked rice and transfer it to a steamer lined with cheesecloth or a clean kitchen towel.
    - Steam the rice over boiling water for 25-30 minutes, or until the grains are tender and cooked through.
3. **Make the Coconut Sauce:**

- o While the rice is steaming, combine the coconut milk, granulated sugar, and salt in a saucepan over medium heat.
- o Stir until the sugar is dissolved and the mixture is smooth. Remove from heat and set aside.
4. **Mix the Rice and Sauce:**
    - o Transfer the cooked sticky rice to a mixing bowl. Gradually pour the coconut sauce over the rice, stirring gently to coat the grains evenly.
5. **Let the Rice Absorb the Sauce:**
    - o Cover the bowl with a clean kitchen towel or plastic wrap and let the rice sit for 15-20 minutes to allow it to absorb the coconut sauce.
6. **Serve:**
    - o Divide the coconut mango sticky rice among serving plates or bowls.
    - o Arrange slices of ripe mango alongside the sticky rice.
7. **Garnish:**
    - o Optionally, sprinkle toasted sesame seeds or shredded coconut over the top for added flavor and texture.

BRAZILIAN AÇAÍ BOWL

- **Servings:** 2
- **Time:** 10 minutes

Ingredients:

- 2 packs frozen unsweetened açaí puree (about 3.5 ounces each)
- 1 ripe banana, sliced

- 1/2 cup frozen mixed berries (such as strawberries, blueberries, raspberries)
- 1/2 cup unsweetened almond milk or coconut water
- 2 tablespoons honey or maple syrup (optional, adjust to taste)
- Toppings: granola, sliced fruits (such as banana, strawberries, kiwi), shredded coconut, chia seeds, nuts, or seeds

Instructions:

1. **Prepare the Açaí Base:**
    - Break the frozen açaí puree packs into chunks and place them in a blender.
    - Add the sliced banana, frozen mixed berries, unsweetened almond milk or coconut water, and honey or maple syrup (if using).
2. **Blend Until Smooth:**
    - Blend the ingredients on high speed until smooth and creamy. If the mixture is too thick, you can add a little more almond milk or coconut water to reach your desired consistency.
3. **Assemble the Açaí Bowls:**
    - Divide the blended açaí mixture evenly between two serving bowls.
4. **Add Toppings:**
    - Top each bowl with your desired toppings, such as granola, sliced fruits, shredded coconut, chia seeds, nuts, or seeds. Get creative and add whatever toppings you enjoy!
5. **Serve:**
    - Serve the Brazilian açaí bowls immediately, and enjoy them with a spoon!

MIDDLE EASTERN ORANGE BLOSSOM RICE PUDDING

- **Servings:** 4
- **Time:** 1 hour 30 minutes

Ingredients:

- 1/2 cup short-grain rice (such as Arborio or sushi rice)
- 4 cups whole milk
- 1/3 cup granulated sugar
- Zest of 1 orange
- 2 tablespoons orange blossom water
- 1/4 teaspoon ground cardamom
- Pinch of salt
- Pistachios or almonds, chopped (for garnish)
- Orange slices (for garnish)

Instructions:

1. **Prepare the Rice:**
    - Rinse the short-grain rice under cold water until the water runs clear. Drain well.
2. **Cook the Rice:**
    - In a medium-sized pot, combine the rinsed rice and whole milk. Bring to a gentle simmer over medium heat, stirring occasionally to prevent the rice from sticking to the bottom of the pot.
3. **Simmer the Rice:**
    - Reduce the heat to low and let the rice simmer gently for about 45-50 minutes, stirring occasionally, until the rice is cooked and the

mixture has thickened to a pudding-like consistency.
4. **Sweeten the Pudding:**
    - Once the rice is cooked and the mixture has thickened, add the granulated sugar, orange zest, orange blossom water, ground cardamom, and a pinch of salt. Stir well to combine.
5. **Continue Cooking:**
    - Let the pudding simmer for an additional 10-15 minutes, stirring occasionally, until the flavors are well incorporated and the pudding has reached your desired consistency. It should be creamy and thick.
6. **Cool and Serve:**
    - Remove the pot from the heat and let the rice pudding cool slightly.
7. **Garnish:**
    - To serve, spoon the orange blossom rice pudding into individual serving bowls. Garnish with chopped pistachios or almonds, and orange slices for a decorative touch.

CHINESE FIVE-SPICE POACHED PEARS

- **Servings:** 4
- **Time:** 1 hour

Ingredients:

- 4 ripe but firm pears
- 4 cups water
- 1 cup granulated sugar
- 2 cinnamon sticks

- 1 star anise
- 1 teaspoon Chinese five-spice powder
- 1 tablespoon lemon juice
- Whipped cream or vanilla ice cream, for serving (optional)
- Chopped nuts or mint leaves, for garnish (optional)

Instructions:

1. **Prepare the Pears:**
    - Peel the pears, leaving the stems intact. Slice a small piece off the bottom of each pear to create a flat surface, allowing them to stand upright.
2. **Poaching Liquid:**
    - In a large pot, combine the water, granulated sugar, cinnamon sticks, star anise, Chinese five-spice powder, and lemon juice. Stir well to dissolve the sugar.
3. **Poach the Pears:**
    - Place the prepared pears upright in the poaching liquid, making sure they are submerged. If necessary, add more water to cover the pears.
4. **Simmer:**
    - Bring the poaching liquid to a gentle simmer over medium heat. Reduce the heat to low, cover the pot, and let the pears simmer for 30-40 minutes, or until they are tender when pierced with a fork.
5. **Cool:**
    - Once the pears are tender, remove the pot from the heat and let the pears cool in the poaching liquid for at least 20-30 minutes.
6. **Serve:**

- Using a slotted spoon, carefully transfer the poached pears to serving plates or bowls.

7. **Reduce Poaching Liquid (Optional):**
   - If desired, bring the poaching liquid to a boil over medium-high heat and let it simmer until reduced by half, creating a syrupy sauce.

8. **Serve with Accompaniments:**
   - Serve the poached pears warm or chilled, drizzled with the reduced poaching liquid and accompanied by whipped cream or vanilla ice cream, if desired.

9. **Garnish:**
   - Garnish the poached pears with chopped nuts or mint leaves for a decorative touch.

MEASUREMENT CONVERSION

Volume Conversions:

- 1 cup = 8 fluid ounces = 240 milliliters
- 1 tablespoon = 3 teaspoons = 15 milliliters
- 1 fluid ounce = 2 tablespoons = 30 milliliters
- 1 quart = 4 cups = 32 fluid ounces = 946 milliliters
- 1 gallon = 4 quarts = 128 fluid ounces = 3.78 liters
- 1 liter = 1,000 milliliters = 33.8 fluid ounces
- 1 milliliter = 0.034 fluid ounces = 0.002 cups

Weight Conversions:

- 1 pound = 16 ounces = 453.592 grams
- 1 ounce = 28.349 grams
- 1 gram = 0.035 ounces = 0.001 kilograms
- 1 kilogram = 1,000 grams = 35.274 ounces = 2.205 pounds

Temperature Conversions:

- To convert from Fahrenheit to Celsius: (°F - 32) / 1.8
- To convert from Celsius to Fahrenheit: (°C * 1.8) + 32

Length Conversions:

- 1 inch = 2.54 centimeters
- 1 foot = 12 inches = 30.48 centimeters
- 1 yard = 3 feet = 36 inches = 91.44 centimeters
- 1 meter = 100 centimeters = 1.094 yards..

www.ingramcontent.com/pod-product-compliance
Ingram Content Group UK Ltd.
Pitfield, Milton Keynes, MK11 3LW, UK
UKHW021321110625
6348UKWH00030B/451